swift

Lorna Hill

wren & rook

High above the hustle
and bustle of the busy
street, Swift huddles
alone in his nest.

He watches other birds
as they chirp and play
outside, wishing they'd
ask him to join them
in the sky. But he's too
nervous to reach out to
them with his wing.

When winter comes, the days
become darker, colder and quieter.
Swift listens for the song of the other birds.
But they have long gone, following the Sun to the south.

Swift wants to stay in his nest, his safe little space.
But he doesn't want to be left behind all alone.

So, bravely, he
uncurls his feathers.

He flaps and he flutters.
He listens to the wind.

And with a strong passing
breeze, Swift takes a great
leap into the sky . . .

He's flying!
He's soaring!

Maybe, if he's quick enough he can catch the other birds.
Swift swoops and he swings, following the Sun.

Swift glides over great oceans and magnificent beasts.

Looking down at the world below, he knows
only birds have such an extraordinary view.

Confident, he soars
higher
and
higher.

He goes
faster
and
faster!

But then, the clouds
begin to rattle . . .

Quick as a blink, the sky bursts into light.

Suddenly, Swift's not flying ... or soaring ...

FLASH!

BANG!

He's
falling . . .

Around him is darkness, just like before.
The forest hums and whistles. Swift is grounded
and helpless, so far from the sky.
He'll never catch up now.

He tries to fly, but his wings flap and flop on the floor.
He tries to run, but his legs are just too small.

Something moves in the bushes.
Swift's eyes dart around, but there's nowhere to hide.

Then out of the bushes tumbles **another swift!**
She's been grounded just like him. They look
at one another with wide, startled eyes.

Perhaps, **together,** they can find a way back to the sky. Nervously, Swift reaches out his wing . . .

The other swift reaches out her wing in return. And, when they are ready, the two birds prepare to take the leap.

One...

two...

three...

Whoosh!
They're flying!
They're soaring!

Once again, the Sun is calling.
But this time something
is different . . .

Swift is not alone.

And through the clouds, where the
Sun is beaming, are hundreds of Swifts.

The flock rushes to welcome Swift and his friend
and together they dance in the blue.

Wing-to-wing, they glide over dusty deserts and lush grasslands. Determined to keep going, they feed and drink on the move, and they never stop to sleep.

Their small bodies are growing tired. But together they are strong, and with each day and night, the Sun draws nearer, the air gets warmer.

At last, they arrive at the place where the Sun sits high in the sky. And as its rays heat up his feathers, where he used to be cold, Swift feels a warmth deep inside. He is safe. He is loved.

He is finally home.

A note from the author

Getting to know swifts first-hand has been a joy and a privilege of mine. I've cared for them when they have been grounded and vulnerable and then witnessed the incredible moment when they take to the sky and come into their own. It is a mesmerising feat. The epic annual journey that they undertake is an inspiration to us all when faced with overwhelming odds.

Lorna Hill

The wonder of swifts

Swifts are great flying experts. They are among the fastest and highest-flying birds of all and make impressively long journeys every year. They are so well suited to being up in the sky that they hardly ever land at all.

Noisy arrivals

Swifts like the ones in this book arrive in Britain and the rest of Europe in spring. They are in a hurry to nest and have babies because they only stay in this part of the world for around three months before flying off again.

Up, up in the air

A young swift can fly the moment it leaves the nest. And what a flight it is! Swifts live almost their whole lives in flight. They catch mosquitoes, flies, butterflies, moths and even tiny spiders on the wing. They may catch 10,000 insects a day, and they even know to avoid stinging insects such as bees and wasps! They collect nesting material in flight, they drink by swooping to take little sips, and they bathe by flying very slowly through rain. Parent swifts sleep in the nest, but for much of the time swifts even sleep high up in the air.

Surviving storms

Sometimes, a storm will knock a swift out of the sky. Usually, it can push off again with its long powerful wings, but sadly young or weak birds may get trapped, unable to launch themselves off the ground.

An incredible journey

Towards the end of summer, the days grow shorter and it's time for swifts to be on the move. They set off on their long migration. They fly fast, up to 111 kilometres an hour. They fly far - up to 800 kilometres a day. They fly high - usually above 50 metres and sometimes over 3 kilmetres high! They stop at their favourite places in West Africa for a few weeks before carrying on to their winter homes, in the tropical forests of Central Africa and the grasslands of East Africa.

Help for swifts

Our Swift is a common swift. Sadly, these swifts are in trouble. There are not as many places for them to nest because modern houses often don't have space for them.

You can help by putting up a special swift nestbox to give them a home.

For my friends and family, particularly my mum and dad,
who have reached out their wings to help me find my way.
All the love x
L.H

First published in Great Britain in 2023 by Wren & Rook

Text and illustration copyright © Lorna Hill, 2023

A CIP catalogue record for this book is available from the British Library.

HB ISBN: 978 1 5263 6523 1   PB ISBN: 978 1 5263 6525 5

Printed and bound in China

1 3 5 7 9 10 8 6 4 2

MIX
Paper from
responsible sources
FSC® C104740

FSC
www.fsc.org

Wren & Rook
An imprint of Hachette Children's Group
Part of Hodder & Stoughton
Carmelite House, 50 Victoria Embankment, London EC4Y 0DZ

An Hachette UK Company
www.hachette.co.uk   www.hachettechildrens.co.uk